lots of
jokes
for kids

lots of jokes for kids

Includes Over 250 Jokes!

ZONDER**kidz**

Our mouths were filled with laughter, our tongues with songs of joy.

Psalm 126:2

ZONDERKIDZ

Lots of Jokes for Kids
Copyright © 2015 by Zonderkidz

This title is also available as a Zondervan ebook.
Visit www.zondervan.com/ebooks.

Requests for information should be addressed to:
Zonderkidz, 3900 Sparks Dr. SE, Grand Rapids, Michigan 49546

ISBN 978-0-310-75057-4

Cover design: Brand Navigation
Interior design: Denise Froehlich

Printed in China

18 19 20 21 22 23 /DSC/ 10 9 8 7 6 5 4 3 2 1

Note to Kids:

Looking for some fun? Want to be silly? Giggle a little? Belly laugh? Then you've come to the right place. This is an awesome collection of really great jokes … OK … so some are corny, some are crazy, and some will make you roll your eyes, but that's what jokes are all about, right?

And this collection is even more special because every joke in here is good for everyone … from your best friends in the whole world Joe and Katey, to mom and dad, to grandma and grandpa, Pastor Joe and Miss Talent, the kindergarten teacher … we mean everyone.

So sit back in that bean bag chair of yours and prepare to be amused.

Table of Contents

Question and Answer.............................9–48

Animal Jokes 49–86

Knock-Knock Jokes 87–112

Bonus Jokes and Riddles................... 113–122

Tongue Twisters 123–127

1

Q & A
Jokes

What did one hat say to the other?
"Stay here, I'll go on ahead."

Why did the cookie cry?
Because his mom was a wafer so long.

What did the big bucket say to the little bucket?
"You look a little pail."

What kind of flowers are on your face?
Tulips.

What do you call a bee having a bad hair day?
A Frisbee.

Why did the cookie go to the hospital?
He was feeling crumby.

What does a ghost wear in the rain?
Boooooots.

Why was the math book upset?
It had a lot of problems.

What has four legs but can't walk?
A chair.

Why did the grasshopper go to the doctor?
Because he was jumpy.

Why did the Oreo go to the dentist?
Because he lost his filling.

Why are ghosts bad liars?
Because you can see right through them.

How do you make an egg roll?
Push it.

What do you call a sad strawberry?
A blueberry.

Why did the lady want wheels on her rocking chair?
So she could rock and roll.

Why was the car so smelly?
It had too much gas.

What goes around the world yet stays in a corner?
A stamp.

Why is it really hot in a stadium after a football game?
All the fans have left.

What did the hot dog say when it won the race?
"I'm the wiener."

Why did the bee get married?
Because she loved her honey.

Why did the tomato turn red?
It saw the salad dressing.

Who can shave six times a day, but still have a beard?
A barber.

How do you make seven an even number?
Take the S out.

Why were the ink spots crying?
Because their mother was in the pen.

What did one flag say to the other flag?
Nothing. It just waved.

What do you get when you stack a bunch of pizzas?
The Leaning Tower of Pizza.

Did you hear about the kid who drank 8 lemonades?
He burped 7 up.

Where do smart hot dogs go?
To the honor roll.

What kind of crackers do firemen like in their soup?
Firecrackers.

Why did the grape stop in the middle of the road?
Because he ran out of juice.

What do you call a fake noodle?

An impasta.

What did the egg say to the person?
"You crack me up."

Which nut sneezes a lot?
A cashew.

What do you get if you eat beans and onions?
Tear gas.

What is brown and sticky?
A stick.

What's black and white and red all over?
A newspaper.

Why shouldn't you play hide and seek with a mountain?
Because it always peeks.

Why was the cook frustrated?
He was running out of thyme.

Why did the policeman stay in bed?
He was undercover.

What did summer say to winter?
"Help. I'm going to fall."

When is a vet the busiest?
When it is raining cats and dogs.

Who stole the soap from the bathtub?
The robber duckie.

What do you call a potato that watches football?
A spec-tator.

What is the ocean's favorite subject?
Current events.

What do you call a wheel that gives speeches?
A spokesman.

What kind of match can't be set on fire?
A tennis match.

What keeps an igloo warm?
Ice-olation.

What do churches and mountains have in common?
They both have steeples.

Which baseball player holds the lemonade?
The pitcher.

When is fishing not relaxing?
When you are the worm.

Why can't you tell jokes on the ice?
It will crack up.

Who is the shortest person in the Bible?
Knee-high-miah.

Why doesn't anyone want to be friends with a clock?
All it does is tock-tock-tock.

Why did the little girl's tooth fall out?
Because it was looth.

What did one eye say to the other?
"Between you and me, something smells."

Why do bees have sticky hair?
They use honeycombs.

Why was 6 afraid of 7?
Because 7 8 9.

Why can't you explain puns to kleptomaniacs?
They always take things, literally.

Why do bankers eat by themselves?
They're loaners.

Why did the computer crash?
It had a bad driver.

What are all of Jaws' clothes made from?
Denim … Denim … Denim, denim, denim.

Why do chicken coops have 2 doors?
If they had 4 doors they would be a chicken sedan.

What do you call a happy cowboy?
A jolly rancher.

What is a vampire's favorite fruit?
A neck-tarine.

What's the best thing to put into pie?
Your teeth.

Why shouldn't you tell an egg a joke?
Because it might crack up.

What do you give a sick lemon?
Lemon-aid.

What time do ducks wake up?
At the quack of dawn.

When do astronauts eat?
At launch time.

What is a ghost's favorite position in soccer?
Ghoul keeper.

What is a cheerleader's favorite color?
Yeller.

What did one volcano say to the other volcano?
"I lava you."

Why didn't the quarter roll down the hill with the nickel?
Because it had more cents.

What kind of lighting did Noah use for the ark?
Floodlights.

Why were the early days of history called the dark ages?
Because there were so many knights.

Why is England the wettest country?
Because the queen has reigned there for years.

Why did the teacher wear sunglasses?
Because his class was so bright.

Why were the teacher's eyes crossed?
She couldn't control her pupils.

Why did the policeman go to the baseball game?
He heard someone had stolen a base.

What do lawyers wear to court?
Lawsuits.

How can you tell the ocean is friendly?
It waves.

When is the moon the heaviest?
When it's full.

What's a tornado's favorite game?
Twister.

What did the ground say to the earthquake?
"You crack me up."

What kind of tree can fit into your hand?
A palm tree.

What makes music on your head?
A headband.

Why did the belt get locked up?
He held up a pair of pants.

What day of the week do potatoes fear most?

Fry-day.

What did the windmill say when she met her favorite movie star?
"Nice to meet you. I'm a BIG FAN."

What did the blanket say to the bed?
"Don't worry, I've got you covered."

Why did the house go to the doctor?
It had window panes.

What has a head and a tail but no body?
A coin.

Where do snowmen go to dance?
A snowball.

What is a witch's favorite subject in school?
Spelling.

What has four wheels and flies?
A garbage truck.

What is easy to get into but hard to get out of?
Trouble.

Why did the poor man sell yeast?
To make some dough.

What did the football coach say to the vending machine?
"Give me my quarterback."

Did you hear about the guy who lost his whole left side?
He's all right now.

What did the baby corn say to the mama corn?
"Where's popcorn?"

What room has no walls?
A mushroom.

What did the man say to the horse when he walked into the room?
"Why the long face?"

How do you communicate with a fish?
You drop it a line.

Where does the president keep his armies?
In his sleevies.

How did the barber win the race?
He knew a short cut.

Why was the man running around his bed?
He wanted to catch up on his sleep.

What rains at the North Pole?
Reindeer.

How did the farmer fix his jeans?
With a cabbage patch.

What is the best way to speak to a monster?
From a long way away.

What do you call cheese that's not yours?
Nacho cheese.

Where do pencils go on vacation?
Pencil-vania.

Why did the boy bring a ladder to school?
He wanted to go to high school.

What do elves learn in school?
The elf-abet.

Why did the girl spread peanut butter on the road?
To go with the traffic jam.

Why don't aliens eat clowns?
Because they taste funny.

Why did the sun go to school?
To get brighter.

What do you call a loony spaceman?
An astronut.

What do clouds wear under their shorts?
Thunderpants.

What did the paper say to the pencil?
"Write on."

Why do bananas put sunscreen on before they go in the sun?
They might peel.

Where would an astronaut park his space ship?

A parking meteor.

Why did the pirate go to the Caribbean?
He wanted some arrr and arrr.

Why couldn't Dracula's wife get to sleep?
Because of his coffin.

Did you hear about the fire at the circus?
It was in tents.

How do you fix a tuba?
With a tuba glue.

How much does a pirate pay for corn?
A buccaneer.

What did one snowman say to the other snowman?
"Hey, do you smell carrots?"

Who did the pharaoh talk to when he was sad?
His mummy.

Why shouldn't you write with a broken pencil?
Because it's pointless.

What did the policeman say to his tummy?
"You're under a vest."

Why does a moon rock taste better than an earth rock?
It's a little meteor.

Why did the cabbage win the race?
Because it was ahead.

What do calendars eat?
Dates.

Why did Cinderella get kicked off the softball team?
Because she ran away from the ball.

What goes up and down but does not move?
Stairs.

Where should a 500 pound alien go?

On a diet.

What did one toilet say to the other?
"You look a bit flushed."

Why did the picture go to jail?
Because it was framed.

What did one wall say to the other wall?
"I'll meet you at the corner."

Why did the skeleton go to the party alone?
Because he had no body to go with him.

What kind of music do mummies listen to?
Wrap.

What washes up on tiny beaches?
Microwaves.

Why did the opera singer go sailing?
She wanted to hit the high C's.

How does the ocean say hello?
It waves.

What is a boxer's favorite drink?
Punch.

What kind of underwear do newspaper reporters wear?
News briefs.

What did Tennessee?
The same thing Arkansas.

How do you make a fire with two sticks?
Make sure one is a match.

What did one penny say to the other penny?
"We make cents together."

How do you cut a wave in half?
Use a sea saw.

Why was the boy sitting on his watch?
Because he wanted to be on time.

Why does the Mississippi River see so well?
It has four eyes.

How do Eskimos make their beds?
With sheets of ice and blankets of snow.

What kind of music do planets sing?
Neptunes.

What is a tree's favorite drink?
Root beer.

Why did the cantaloupe jump in the lake?
Because it wanted to be a watermelon.

What gets wetter the more it dries?
A towel.

What kind of nails do carpenters hate hammering?
Fingernails.

Why was the broom late?
It over-swept.

What do you call a banana that has been cut in half?
A banana split.

Why did the golfer wear two pairs of pants?
In case he got a hole in one.

Why did the reporter walk into the ice cream shop?
Because he wanted a scoop.

What is the tallest building in any city?
A library, because it has so many stories.

Why did the student eat his homework?
The teacher told him it was a piece of cake.

Why did the farmer cross the road?
To catch the chicken.

Where does seaweed look for a job?
In the kelp wanted ads.

What's the slipperiest country?
Greece.

What is the fiercest flower in the garden?
The tiger lily.

Why do dragons sleep during the day?
So they can fight knights.

What do postal workers do when they're mad?
They stamp their feet.

Why do bicycles fall over?
Because they are two-tired.

How can you tell that a train just went by?
It left its tracks.

What did the laundryman say to the impatient customer?
"Keep your shirt on."

What's a golfer's favorite letter?
Tee.

Why are the floors of basketball courts always so damp?
The players dribble.

Why was everyone so tired on April 1st?
They had just finished a March of 31 days.

What is the world's longest punctuation mark?
A hundred yard dash.

What is it that even the most careful person overlooks?
Her nose.

Why did Mozart get rid of his chickens?
They kept saying, "Bach, Bach."

What starts with E, ends with E and only has one letter?
An envelope.

Why did the robber take a bath before he stole from the bank?
He wanted to make a clean get away.

Why did the scarecrow win the Nobel Prize?
Because he was out standing in his field.

Why are traffic lights never ready on time?
Because they take too long to change.

What did Mars say to Saturn?
"Give me a ring sometime."

How do trains hear?
Through their engineers.

Why did the basketball player go to jail?
Because he shot the ball.

What is black, white, green, and bumpy?
A pickle wearing a tuxedo.

What did the ceiling say to the chandelier?
"You're the bright spot in my life."

Why did the sun go to school?
To get brighter.

What two things can you not have for breakfast?
Lunch and dinner.

Why did the tree go to the dentist?
It needed a root canal.

What new crop did the farmer plant?
Beets me.

What did the spider do on the computer?
Made a website.

What do you call an underwater spy?
James Pond.

What do you get when you cross a computer and a lifeguard?
A screensaver.

What kind of plates do they use on Venus?
Flying saucers.

How does the Easter bunny stay in shape?
Lots of eggsercise.

What did Delaware?
A New Jersey.

Have you heard the rumor about the butter?
I better not tell you, it might spread.

2

Animal Jokes

What goes snap, crackle, squeak?
Mice Krispies.

What kind of animal should you never play cards with?
A cheetah.

What do you call a bear with no teeth?
A gummy bear.

Why do fish swim in salt water?
Because pepper makes them sneeze.

What dog can jump higher than a building?
Any dog—buildings can't jump.

What's black and white and makes a lot of noise?
A zebra playing drums.

What do you get when you cross a chicken and a Chihuahua?
Pooched eggs.

What animal needs to wear a wig?
A bald eagle.

What's the best way to catch a fish?
Have someone throw it to you.

What kind of music do frogs like to dance to?
Hip Hop.

Why does a rhino have so many wrinkles?
Because he's hard to iron.

What color do cats like?
Purrrrrrple.

Where do cows get their medicine?
From the farmacy.

What do you call a sleeping bull?
A bulldozer.

Why did the little bird go to the hospital?
To get tweet-ment.

What do you get from a pampered cow?
Spoiled milk.

What did the buffalo say to his kid when he dropped him off at school?
"Bison."

Why are horses such lousy dancers?
They have two left feet.

What do you get when you cross a parrot and a centipede?
A walkie-talkie.

What did the duck say when he bought lipstick?

"Put it on my bill."

What is gray, has four legs, a tail, and a trunk?
A mouse on vacation.

Why did the monkey fall out of the tree?
Because it was dead.

What do you call a porcupine that doesn't move?
A cactus.

What did the horse say when its food ran away?
"Hay."

What do you call a grizzly bear caught in the rain?
A drizzly bear.

What do you call a dog that creates books?
A pup-lisher.

What do you call a flying ape?
A hot-air baboon.

Why can't a leopard ever win at hide and seek?
Because it is always spotted.

What do you call a really jumpy dog?
A kanga-roof.

What do you do when you are surrounded by lions, tigers, and cheetahs?
Get off the carousel.

What bird is good to have at every meal?
A swallow.

What do you get when you cross a mouse with a squid?
An eektopus.

What time is it when an elephant sits on the fence?
Time to fix the fence.

Why did the chicken cross the playground?
To get to the other slide.

What do cows say in space?
"Mooooo-n."

What do you use to groom a rabbit?
A hare brush.

Why did the leopard wear a striped shirt?
So she wouldn't be spotted.

What part of a turkey is musical?
The drumstick.

Why are cats so good at video games?
Because they have nine lives.

What do you get when you cross a computer with an elephant?
Lots of memory.

Why couldn't the pony sing?
Because he was a little hoarse.

What color socks do bears wear?
They don't wear socks, they have bear feet.

Why did the cat get 100 percent on its test?
It was purrfect.

What's black and white, black and white, and black and white?
A panda bear rolling down a hill.

What is the biggest ant in the world?
An eleph-ant.

Why did the bee go to the doctor?
Because she had hives.

What do you get if you cross a grizzly bear and a harp?
A bear-faced lyre.

Why are frogs so happy?
Because they eat what bugs them.

Why did the kid throw the butter out the window?
To see the butter fly.

What do you call bears with no ears?
B.

Why didn't the teddy bear eat his lunch?

Because he was stuffed.

What do you call it when it rains chickens and ducks?
Foul weather.

Where do milkshakes come from?
Nervous cows.

What do you call a pig that knows karate?
A pork chop.

Why do seagulls fly over the sea?
Because if they flew over the bay they would be called bagels.

Where does a peacock go when it loses its tail?
A re-tail store.

What kind of bird can carry the most weight?
The crane.

What do polar bears eat for lunch?
Ice berg-ers.

Why was the baby ant confused?
Because all of his uncles were ants.

What do you get when you cross a sheep and a honeybee?
Bah-humbug.

What do you get if you cross a parrot with a shark?
A bird that will talk your ear off.

What steps do you take if a tiger is running towards you?
Big ones.

What is black and white and red all over?
A panda bear with a sunburn.

What do cats eat for breakfast?
Mice Krispies.

What's the nickname for someone who put her right hand in the mouth of a lion?
Lefty.

Why didn't the butterfly go to the dance?
Because it was a moth ball.

Why can't you shock cows?
They've herd it all.

What did one frog say to the other?
"Time's sure fun when you're having flies."

Why was the mother firefly unhappy?
Because her children weren't that bright.

How do you plan a space party?
You planet early.

Why didn't the boy believe the tiger?
He thought it was a lion.

What is black and white and eats like a horse?
A zebra.

When is it very bad luck to see a black cat?
When you're a mouse.

What did the farmer call the cow that had no milk?
An udder failure.

What do you get if you cross a cocker spaniel, a poodle, and a rooster?

Cockerpoodledoo.

Where do cows go for entertainment?
To the moo-vies.

What kind of horses go out after dark?
Nightmares.

What do you get when you cross a walrus with a bee?
A wallaby.

What's white, furry, and shaped like a tooth?
A molar bear.

What do you get when you cross an octopus and a cow?
An animal that can milk itself.

What happened to the lost cattle?
Nobody's herd.

Why do bears have fur coats?
Because they look silly wearing jackets.

What do you get if you cross a teddy bear with a pig?
A teddy boar.

Which side of a cheetah has the most spots?
The outside.

Why is a horse like a wedding?
They both need a groom.

What do you call it when a dinosaur crashes his car?
A tyrannosaurus wrecks.

What do farmer birds say while they are harvesting?
"Twheat. Too-eat."

What do you get if you cross a kangaroo and a snake?
A jump rope.

How do teddy bears keep their den cool in summer?
They use bear conditioning.

How do bees get to school?
By school buzz.

Why do ducks have flat feet?
To stamp out forest fires.

Why do elephants have flat feet?
To stamp out flaming ducks.

What time is it when ten tigers are chasing after you?
Ten after one.

What is smarter than a talking bird?
A spelling bee.

What does a snail say when he's riding on a turtle's back?
"Weeeeeee."

Where do sheep get their wool cut?
At the baa-baa shop.

What do you call a deer with no eye?
No idear.

What did one shark say to the other while eating a clownfish?
"This tastes funny."

What was T. rex's favorite number?
Eight.

How does a lion like his meat?
Roar.

How do you get a rhinoceros to stop charging?
Take away his credit card.

What do you call an elephant in a phone booth?
Stuck.

How many tickles does it take to make a squid laugh?

Ten-tickles.

Why wouldn't the shrimp share his treasure?
Because he was a little shellfish.

What do you call a sheep covered in chocolate?
A chocolate baaaaaar.

What bird steals from the rich to give to the poor?
Robin Hood.

What did the mother bee say to the baby bee?
"Behive yourself."

Why did the two boa constrictors get married?
Because they had a crush on each other.

What do you call a fish with no eyes?
Fsh.

Where do salmon keep their money?
In a riverbank.

Why did the dog go to court?
Because he got a barking ticket.

Why did the bubble gum cross the road?
Because it was stuck to the chicken's foot.

What is a crocodile's favorite drink?
Gator-ade.

Why can't you find a good animal doctor?
Animals have a hard time getting into medical school.

How do you catch a squirrel?
Climb up a tree and act like a nut.

Why did the salamander feel lonely?
Because he was newt to the area.

What do you get if a chicken walks across the road, rolls in mud, and crosses back again?
A dirty double crosser.

What is a frog's favorite warm drink?
Hot croako.

What lion never roars?
A dandelion.

What has 12 legs, 6 eyes, 3 tails, and can't see?
Three blind mice.

What's big and gray with horns?
An elephant marching band.

Why do birds fly south?
Because it's too far to walk.

Why do you need a license for a dog but not for a cat?
Cats can't drive.

What do you call a really big ant?
A giANT.

What goes dot-dot-croak, dot-dash-croak?
Morse Toad.

What is a llama's favorite drink?
Llama-nade.

How do you get an elephant into a refrigerator?
Just open the door and stick him in.

How do you put a giraffe into a refrigerator?
First you have to take the elephant out, then you can put the giraffe in.

If all of the animals had a meeting, which one would be missing?
The giraffe, because he's still in the fridge.

Where does a dog park his car?
In a barking lot or a grrrage.

What did the orangutan call his wife?
His prime-mate.

Why did the crab go to prison?
Because he kept pinching things.

Which dog can tell time?
A watchdog.

What do ducks watch on TV?
Duckumentaries.

Where do orcas hear music?
Orca-stras.

Where do rabbits go when they are sick?
To the hopital.

Why do bees hum?
Because they don't know the words.

What do you name an elephant hiding in a pile of leaves?
Russell.

What do you call a thieving alligator?
A crookodile.

Where do you get frogs' eggs?
At the spawn shop.

What snakes are found on cars?
Windshield vipers.

What happened to the cat that swallowed a ball of wool?
She had mittens.

When you catch your dog eating a dictionary, what should you do?
Take the words right out of his mouth.

How do oysters call their friends?
On shell phones.

What has four legs and goes "Oom, Oom"?
A cow walking backwards.

What do you call a cold dog sitting on a bunny?
A chili dog on a bun.

What mouse was a Roman emperor?
Julius Cheeser.

How do porcupines kiss each other?
Very carefully.

What should you do if you find a jaguar asleep on your bed?
Sleep on the sofa.

What animals are on legal documents?
Seals.

Eleven dogs shared one umbrella, yet none got wet. How did they manage?
It wasn't raining.

What do you call a fly without wings?
A walk.

What happened when the owl lost his voice?
He didn't give a hoot.

How do you make a goldfish old?
Take away the g.

How many skunks does it take to stink up a house?
A phew.

What's gray and squeaky and hangs around in caves?
Stalagmice.

Why can't a leopard hide?

Because it's always spotted.

How does a dog stop a video?
He presses the paws button.

What is the difference between an elephant and a flea?
An elephant can have fleas but a flea can't have elephants.

How do two snails fight?
They slug it out.

What kind of math do birds like?
Owlgebra.

Why did the dog cross the road twice?
He was trying to fetch a boomerang.

What's worse than raining cats and dogs?
Hailing taxis.

What do you call two spiders who just got married?
Newlywebs.

What do you call a crying camel?
A humpback wail.

Why did the turkey cross the road?
To prove he wasn't chicken.

How do you keep an elephant in suspense?
I'll tell you tomorrow.

What do chicken families do on Saturday afternoons?
They go on peck-nics.

Where do horses live?
In the neigh-borhood.

What do you give a sick pig?
Oink-ment.

What do camels use to hide themselves?
Camelflage.

What is the best way to communicate with a fish?
Drop it a line.

What did the judge say when the skunk walked into the court room?
Odor in the court!

What do you get if you cross an elephant with a kangaroo?
Big holes all over Australia.

What's orange and sounds like a parrot?
A carrot.

Why did the dinosaur cross the road?
Because chickens weren't alive yet.

How does a penguin build its house?
Igloos it together.

Why are snakes hard to fool?
They have no legs to pull.

What do you call an owl with a deep voice?
A growl.

What do whales eat?
Fish and ships.

Which fish can perform operations?
A sturgeon.

What do you call a dinosaur that never gives up?
A try and try-ceratops.

If fruit comes from a fruit tree, where does turkey come from?
A poul-tree.

Why did the poor dog chase his own tail?
He was trying to make both ends meet.

What key won't open any door?
A monkey.

What do angry rodents send each other at the holidays?
Cross-mouse cards.

Where do tough chickens come from?
Hard-boiled eggs.

What do fish take to stay healthy?
Vitamin sea.

What do you get if you cross a dog with a telephone?
A golden receiver.

When does a horse talk?
Whinny wants to.

What did the sardine call the submarine?
A can of people.

What do you call a show full of lions?
The mane event.

Why do male deer need braces?
Because they have buck teeth.

What part of a fish weighs the most?
Its scales.

What is a frog's favorite year?

Leap year.

Where do birds invest their money?
In the stork market.

Why did the snowman call his dog "Frost"?
Because Frost bites.

What do you get from an Alaskan cow?
Ice cream.

What kind of mouse does not eat, drink, or even walk?
A computer mouse.

What is the strongest creature in the sea?
A mussel.

3

Knock-Knock Jokes

Knock, knock.
Who's there?
A-bott.
A-bott who?
A-bott time you answered the door.

Knock, knock.
Who's there?
Phillip.
Phillip who?
Fill up your pool. I wanna take a dip.

Knock, knock.
Who's there?
Kook.
Kook who?
Don't call me cuckoo.

Knock, knock.
Who's there?
Cowsgo.
Cowsgo who?
No they don't, cows go moo.

Knock, knock.
Who's there?
You know.
You know who?
Ah. It's You-know-who.

Knock, knock.
Who's there?
Owls.
Owls who?
That's right, owls whoooooooo.

Knock, knock.
Who's there?
I eat mop.
I eat mop who?
You do what??

Knock, knock.
Who's there?
Lettuce.
Lettuce who?
Let us in, it's cold out here.

Knock, knock.
Who's there?
Leaf.
Leaf who?
Leaf me alone.

Knock, knock.
Who's there?
Jo.
Jo who?
Jo King.

Knock, knock.
Who's there?
A herd.
A herd who?
A herd you were home, so I came over.

Knock, knock.
Who's there?
Harry.
Harry who?
Harry up and you will find out.

Knock, knock.
Who's there?
Iva.
Iva who?
I've a sore hand from knocking.

Knock, knock.
Who's there?
Nobel.
Nobel who?
No bell, that's why I knocked.

Knock, knock.
Who's there?
Woo.
Woo who?
Don't get so excited, it's just a joke.

Knock, knock.
Who's there?
Anita.
Anita who?
Anita to borrow a pencil.

Knock, knock.
Who's there?
Dozen.
Dozen who?
Dozen anybody want to let me in?

Knock, knock.
Who's there?
Sing.
Sing who?
Whoooooo.

Knock, knock.
Who's there?
Dwayne.
Dwayne who?
Dwayne the bathtub, it's overflowing.

Knock, knock.
Who's there?
Lena.
Lena who?
Lena little closer and I'll tell you.

Knock, knock.
Who's there?
Alaska.
Alaska who?
Alaska another question now ...

Knock, knock.
Who's there?
Ohio.
Ohio who?
Oh, how are you doing?

Knock, knock.
Who's there?
Avenue.
Avenue who?
Avenue knocked on this door before?

Knock, knock.
Who's there?
Cook.
Cook who?
Stop making bird noises and open the door.

Knock, knock.
Who's there?
Russian.
Russian who?
Stop rushin' me.

Knock, knock.
Who's there?
Adore.
Adore who?
Adore is between us. Open up.

Knock, knock.
Who's there?
Mikey.
Mikey who?
Mikey doesn't fit in the hole.

Knock, knock.
Who's there?
Interrupting cow.
Interrupting c—
Mooooo.

Knock, knock.
Who's there?
Banana.
Banana who?
Knock, knock.
Who's there?
Banana.
Banana who?
Knock, knock.
Who's there?
Orange.
Orange who?
Orange you glad I didn't say banana?

Knock, knock.
Who's there?
Radio.
Radio who?
Radio not here I come.

Knock, knock.
Who's there?
A little old lady.
A little old lady who?
I didn't know you could yodel.

Knock, knock.
Who's there?
Cargo.
Cargo who?
Car go "beep, beep, vroom, vroom."

Knock, knock.
Who's there?
Beets.
Beets who?
Beets me.

Knock, knock.
Who's there?
Lion.
Lion who?
Lion on your doorstep, open up.

Knock, knock.
Who's there?
Kirtch.
Kirtch who?
God bless you.

Knock, knock.
Who's there?
Kent.
Kent who?
Kent you tell by my voice?

Knock, knock.
Who's there?
Tank.
Tank who?
You're welcome.

Knock, knock.
Who's there?
Luke.
Luke who?
Luke through the peephole and find out.

Knock, knock.
Who's there?
Jess.
Jess who?
Jess me and my shadow.

Knock, knock.
Who's there?
Wooden shoe.
Wooden shoe who?
Wooden shoe like to hear another joke?

Knock, knock.
Who's there?
Arfur.
Arfur who?
Arfur got.

Knock, knock.
Who's there?
Isabel.
Isabel who?
Isabel working? I had to knock.

Knock, knock.
Who's there?
Barbie.
Barbie who?
Barbie Q. Chicken.

Knock, knock.
Who's there?
Utah.
Utah who?
U talking to me?

Knock, knock.
Who's there?
Nana.
Nana who?
Nana your business.

Knock, knock.
Who's there?
Kiwi.
Kiwi who?
Kiwi go to the store?

Knock, knock.
Who's there?
Amy.
Amy who?
Amy 'fraid I've forgotten.

Knock, knock.
Who's there?
Amos.
Amos who?
A mosquito.

Knock, knock.
Who's there?
Anudder.
Anudder who?
Anudder mosquito.

Knock, knock.
Who's there?
Ya.
Ya who?
Wow. You sure are excited to see me.

Knock, knock.
Who's there?
Turnip.
Turnip who?
Turnip the volume, it's too quiet.

Knock, knock.
Who's there?
Ketchup.
Ketchup who?
Ketchup with you soon.

Knock, knock.
Who's there?
Police.
Police who?
Police hurry up, it's chilly outside.

Knock, knock.
Who's there?
Handsome.
Handsome who?
Handsome money through the keyhole and I'll tell you.

Knock, knock.
Who's there?
Goat.
Goat who?
Goat to the door and find out.

Knock, knock.
Who's there?
A little boy.
A little boy who?
A little boy who can't reach the doorbell.

Knock, knock.
Who's there?
Justin.
Justin who?
Just in the neighborhood, thought I would drop by.

Knock, knock.
Who's there?
Abby.
Abby who?
Abby birthday to you.

Knock, knock.
Who's there?
Beef.
Beef who?
Before I get cold, you'd better let me in.

Knock, knock.
Who's there?
Crab.
Crab who?
Crab me a snack, please.

Knock, knock.
Who's there?
Ben.
Ben who?
Ben knocking for ten minutes.

Knock, knock.
Who's there?
Emma.
Emma who?
Emma bit cold out here, could you let me in?

Knock, knock.
Who's there?
You be.
You be who?
You be a pal and bring me a cookie.

Knock, knock.
Who's there?
Howard.
Howard who?
Howard I know?

Knock, knock.
Who's there?
Who.
Who who?
Are you an owl?

Knock, knock.
Who's there?
Maya.
Maya who?
Maya name is Dan.

Knock, knock.
Who's there?
Dewey.
Dewey who?
Dewey have to keep telling silly jokes?

Knock, knock.
Who's there?
Abe.
Abe who?
ABE C D E F G H...

Knock, knock.
Who's there?
Alex.
Alex who?
Alex-plain later.

Knock, knock.
Who's there?
Ivana.
Ivana who?
Ivana come in.

Knock, knock.
Who's there?
Doris.
Doris who?
Doris locked, that's why I knocked.

Knock, knock.
Who's there?
Champ.
Champ who?
Champ poo your hair—it's dirty.

Knock, knock.
Who's there?
Tiss.
Tiss who?
Tiss who is good for blowing your nose.

Knock, knock.
Who's there?
Dishes.
Dishes who?
Dishes me, who are you?

Knock, knock.
Who's there?
Spell.
Spell who?
W-H-O

Knock, knock.
Who's there?
Carl.
Carl who?
Car'll get you there faster than a bike.

Knock, knock.
Who's there?
Norma Lee.
Norma Lee who?
Norma Lee I don't go around knocking on doors, but I just had to meet you.

Knock, knock.
Who's there?
Gorilla.
Gorilla who?
Gorilla me a steak.

Knock, knock.
Who's there?
Olive.
Olive who?
Olive right next door.

Knock, knock.
Who's there?
Adam.
Adam who?
Adam my way, I'm coming through.

Knock, knock.
Who's there?
Ice cream.
Ice cream who?
Ice cream if you don't let me in.

Knock, knock.
Who's there?
Boo.
Boo who?
Don't cry—it's just a knock-knock joke.

Knock, knock.
Who's there?
Oswald.
Oswald who?
Oswald my bubble gum.

Knock, knock.
Who's there?
Cash.
Cash who?
I knew you were a nut.

Knock, knock.
Who's there?
Figs.
Figs who?
Figs the doorbell, it's broken.

Knock, knock.
Who's there?
Knock, knock.
Who's there?
You're supposed to say "knock knock who."

Knock, knock.
Who's there?
Broccoli.
Broccoli who?
Broccoli doesn't have a last name, silly.

Knock, knock.
Who's there?
Alpaca.
Alpaca who?
Alpaca the trunk, you pack the suitcase.

Knock, knock.
Who's there?
Doughnut.
Doughnut who?
Doughnut ask, it's a secret.

Knock, knock.
Who's there?
Impatient pirate.
Impatient p—
ARRRRRRRRRR.

Knock, knock.
Who's there?
Opportunity.
Opportunity who?
Opportunity doesn't knock twice.

Knock, knock.
Who's there?
Otto.
Otto who?
Otto know. I've got amnesia.

4

Bonus Jokes and Riddles

A man runs into a hospital and yells, "Help. I'm shrinking." One of the nurses sits the man down. "We're very busy here today sir, you're going to have to be a little patient."

There were two cows in a field. The first cow said "moo" and the second cow said "baaaa." The first cow asked the second cow, "Why did you say baaaa?" The second cow said, "I'm learning a foreign language."

A man walks into his doctor's office with a carrot in his ear and a banana in his nose. He asks, "What's wrong, doc?" The doctor replies, "You're not eating right."

Farmers earn a meager celery, come home beet, and just want to read the pepper, turn-ip the covers, en-dive into bed.

I wondered why the baseball was getting bigger. Then it hit me.

Where are cars most likely to get flat tires?
At forks in the road.

What kind of band can't play music?
A rubber band.

What do hockey players and magicians have in common?
Both do hat tricks.

What happened when two silkworms got into a race?
It ended in a tie.

Why was there thunder and lightning in the lab?
The scientists were brainstorming.

How do you catch a unique rabbit?
Unique up on it.

How do you catch a tame rabbit?
Tame way, unique up on it.

Why was the nose tired?
Because it had been running all day.

Why are pirates pirates?
Because they just RRRRRR.

What did the hamburger give his sweetheart?
An onion ring.

What do monkeys sing at Christmas?
Jungle Bells.

Why do dogs run in circles?
Because it's hard to run in squares.

What goes up but never comes down?
Your age.

What kind of apple has a short temper?
A crab apple.

How do you paint a rabbit purple?
With purple hare spray.

When does it rain money?
When there is change in the weather.

What did the fork say to the knife?
"You're looking sharp."

What are the strongest days of the week?
Saturday and Sunday. Every other day is a weekday.

What did zero say to eight?
"Nice belt."

What do you call a great dog detective?

Sherlock Bones.

1. I'm tall when I'm young and I'm short when I'm old. What am I?

2. How can a pocket be empty and still have something in it?

3. In a one-story pink house, there was a pink lady, a pink cat, a pink fish, a pink couch, a pink table, a pink telephone, a pink toilet. Everything was pink. What color were the stairs?

4. What goes around and around a tree but never goes into the wood?

5. What is put on a table and cut, but never eaten?

(1. A candle; 2. It can have a hole in it; 3. It's a one-story house—there are no stairs; 4. The tree's bark; 5. A deck of cards)

1. A dad and his son were in an accident. Two ambulances came and took them to different hospitals. The man's son was in the operating room and the doctor said, "I can't operate on you. You're my son." How is that possible?

2. You throw away the outside and cook the inside, then eat the outside and throw away the inside. What is it?

3. What is full of holes but still holds water?

4. What appears twice in a week and once in a year but never in a day?

5. Where do you find roads without vehicles, forests without trees, and cities without houses?

(1. The doctor is his mom; 2. Corn on the cob: you throw away the husk, cook and eat the kernels, and throw away the cob; 3. A sponge; 4. The letter E; 5. On a map)

1. What has a tongue, cannot walk on its own, but goes lots of places?

2. What has to be broken before you can use it?

3. Two mothers and two daughters go to a pet store and buy three dogs. Each person gets her own dog. How is this possible?

4. What belongs to you but is used more by others?

5. What is as light as a feather, but even the world's strongest man couldn't hold it for more than a few minutes?

(1. A shoe; 2. An egg; 3. There are only three people: a grandmother (who is also a mother), a mother (who is also a daughter), and a daughter; 4. Your name; 5. His breath)

1. A horse is tied to a 10-foot-long rope. The horse wants to get some water that is 20 feet away. The horse gets the water easily. How can he do this?

2. It's been around for millions of years, but it's no more than a month old. What is it?

3. You walk into a room with a match, a lamp, a candle, and a fireplace. Which do you light first?

4. What has a thumb and four fingers but is not alive?

5. What has a face and two hands but no arms or legs?

(1. The other end of the rope isn't tied to anything; 2. The moon; 3. The match; 4. A glove; 5. A clock.)

5 Tongue Twisters

Greek grapes.

Chop shops stock chops.

Fred fed Ted bread, and Ted fed Fred bread.

If one doctor doctors another doctor, does the doctor who doctors the doctor doctor the doctor the way the doctor he is doctoring doctors? Or does he doctor the doctor the way the doctor who doctors doctors?

Please pay promptly.

Shredded Swiss cheese.

If two witches were watching two watches, which witch would watch which watch?

Six slippery snails slowly slid seaward.

I thought a thought. But the thought I thought wasn't the thought I thought I thought.

If the thought I thought I thought had been the thought I thought, I wouldn't have thought so much.

Eleven owls licked eleven little licorice lollipops.

The blue bluebird blinks.

Red leather, yellow leather.

A proper copper coffee pot.

Irish wristwatch.

A good cook could cook as many cookies as a good cook who could cook cookies.

Lesser leather never weathered wetter weather better.

Forty-three free throws.

Can you imagine an imaginary menagerie manager imagining managing an imaginary menagerie?

The big bug bit the little beetle, but the little beetle bit the big bug back.

Old oily Ollie oils old oily autos.

Cows graze in groves on grass which grows in grooves in groves.

Seventy-seven benevolent elephants.

Clean clams crammed in clean cans.

Double bubble gum, bubbles double.

I saw a saw that could out saw any other saw I ever saw.

Are our oars oak?

We surely shall see the sunshine soon.

Moose munching much mush.

Lots of Knock-Knock Jokes for Kids

New from Zonderkidz, here's a collection of knock-knock jokes that's both hilarious and wholesome. *Lots of Knock-Knock Jokes for Kids* is sure to send every kid you know to her knees in a breath-stealing, side-splitting, uncontrollable fit of giggles—it's *that* funny.